The Stripping Point

The Stripping Point

Brian Henry

Counterpath Press
Denver, Colorado
2007

Counterpath Press
Denver, Colorado
www.counterpathpress.org

Thanks to Ernie Hilbert at *NowCulture* for publishing the
first thirteen parts of "The Stripping Point" (under the title
"Olfactory") as a hypertext series. Parts of the poem also appeared
in *Columbia Poetry Review*. Parts of "More Dangerous Than
Dying" have appeared or are forthcoming in *Coconut*,
H_NGM_N, *Kulture Vulture*, and *Octopus*.

Printed in Canada

Distributed by Small Press Distribution, www.spdbooks.org

Library of Congress Cataloging-in-Publication Data

Henry, Brian, 1972–
    The stripping point / Brian Henry.
        p.   cm.
    ISBN 978-1-933996-01-1 (pbk. : alk. paper)
I. Title.

PS3608.E566S77 2007
811'.6—DC22

                                              2006037257

Contents

for JW

More Dangerous Than Dying

I was living . . . on the edge of a landscape of vast shame.
—Don DeLillo, *White Noise*

The long and short of it
transferred
to another department

we never get the gist

Just as knowledge stands before us
ready to render us
wise

it pushes ahead of me
wheedles its way to the top

You have been this way
and I am following.

A thing is delivered
to your In-basket

carbon-copy to me

The official words forlorn

You whistle over the din

                          a tune I cannot catch

On the cusp   our routine location

We hold hands
by the water cooler

I feed my copy to you

                    You press yours
                    against my tonsils

did flaunt
every asset we had

Twice-worn shirts
waiting for the laundromat

"Your job is safe"
my threadbare consolation

"No matter what
we'll have each other"
my appraisal

You roll and pull
the cord

My pupils hold
the dark until morning

Late September is a choking furnace.

The sun tries to roll its way over us
and strike into the distance

a missile with no trail
no final destination

We tilt toward the kitchen
find no light to go by

Cat hair pools
connects under the bed

The wood of the floor molds to my spine
the bed holds its place in the corner

The sun tries to roll its way
over us

We stir and pivot
stay our course   lightless

a little mission
fraught with anchors

You propose a walk
through the park
to dispel the malaise
plaguing the house
all autumn

My counter-proposal   to scour the fridge
a task with untold
salutary effects on the spirit

Something rather cathartic
rather
in its opposition
to this inertia

There is too much air in the air.

The office party was a carnal affair

The elevator between floors
we descended three flights
for the room key

Ed from Accounting
with his tequila

Licking slamming sucking
to a free continental breakfast

Excess punishes me, never forgives.

A glancing blow
that hurts less than it threatens

I stare at my slide rule
back-and-forth it
until I blister

suffering my eye to follow

You are not answering

Your intern routes my calls
to Inspections
where Ivan explains
the need for a 96% acceptance rate
and the unlikelihood of profit
or Xmas bonuses
with anything less

I doodle
hang up
call again
and Ivan explains
the need for a 96% acceptance rate
and the unlikelihood of profit
or Xmas bonuses
with anything less

I call
ask for Ivan

Reinhart in Heat Treating
hellos over the furnaces

so radiant in the back
ground

a clear human voice
I have been afraid of ever since

Incompetent drifter

Preternatural leave-taker

You spread yourself
across my landscape
with a tacit promise
to stay for a while
but just as quickly
as you lay yourself out
for inspection
you pick yourself up
and take yourself away
away from me
and this dream of mine
a dream that has to do
with flying   flying
low over a field of corn

or is it soybeans?

Solace is found in sameness

I allow myself
a quiet moment

head in arms on desk

freshly cut trees
jerking as they ascend

Amidst this haste and filth

Pacing the hall outside
the Director's office

the plaque with his name
misspelled
catches my every move

The call to order
every Thursday
a tradition that excludes
in its lack of exclusivity

My skills   spatial logic
                             synapse analysis
                             reaction times and all
                             but the most complex
                             of calculations

Deserving of something
more   something
nobler   or inflationary at least
I pace   pause
crack the door to a sliver

The Director has a hold
on himself
modem squawking
in time to the beat

"I," I mused, "yes, I"

The conflagration seemed severe

Our first visit to church in four years
we sat deep in the congregation

As we went for our wafers
the line stopped and scattered
people piled onto each other
toppling pews   picking children
                    from the floor

I strained to see the priest's reaction
you grabbing my hand   mouthing
screaming probably
about fire or smoke   some poor person
needing rescue or resuscitation
your mouth twisted
the crowns on your molars
your new eyes   not looking at me
or even through me
eyes like water   like smoke
                    from a candle

No   like smoke from a wood stove

The one we used on vacation last winter

The light at least was not to be dismissed.

The significance of the difference
between the tip as calculated
and the tip as left on the table
becomes a wedge between us

I beg to focus on weighty things

the need for a 96% acceptance rate
the softball game on Saturday
the lunar eclipse at 9:19

Your mouth shatters when I swat it

On and on and on
my apologies scatter
and lift

I repeat things in order to feel them.

"I want more mystery in my life

not projected   not refracted

Not a veil   Not a mesh
Not barbed wire

But something   a way to say
'This has been done without a clear reason'
without a clear reason"

NOTHING is exactly what we do.

Impasses impasses
            the built-in excuses
            we whisper to ourselves
            in the shower each morning

Passionate one   confront your insecurities
            and insufficiencies

Looking in the mirror won't work
nor will a posture of prayer

You hit the snooze bar for another seven minutes of sleep
sit up   stand up   head for the shower
shower   put on your face   dry your hair   dress
note the forecast   slide your keys from the counter
open the back door   pass through   close it
start your Accord   back out   drive to the plant

What is anything but dying?

This this
we so
languidly protest
against

The no, not, never,
not even, nothing of the day.
The nothing, nada, no thing,
not now of morning.

Linen closet fantasies
perpetuate the impossible

an illogical progression
from this to that   and back again

The dishes dry   the rag damp

Ammonia a way of life here
it precludes the intrusion of leisure

or any manifesto

into our days of such-and-such
and somnambulance

What happened to the pleasure principle?

Predicting the next time
or even this time   unfulfilled luster

The lot is cast   bets made

My chatter is meant to distract you from my ignorance.

A captured document

                              a card
                              in green ink
                              You & me
                              with a bottle of Beam

It is filed by a gloveless hand
under Q
the folder of secrets and spells

"Just a matter of days
before they trace the hand
back to this office"

outside, melting white paper

The weather holding

              not to say that anything actually rested
              in its hands
              just that a pattern
              retained a semblance of constancy

we drive to the driving range

Borrowed and bent clubs the norm

the wind accentuates your slice
negates my incurable hook

This outing   this celebration
complete with new apparel

the result of your stumbling
upon the bit that "insanity" rhymes

with "vanity"

Nothing to compress the space between

The stench stinks.

Leisure activities add weight
a hiccup for the deliberate motions

We know no destination
bothered us nights
so let us praise those
who work with their hands
whatever their products wreak

Perhaps bloodshot eyes
would take us where we want to go

You go to bed a failure and rise a saint

"Casual drifter
the wheels roll
us to a new state
of belonging
　　　　　and that helmet . . . "

Perhaps it's not sight
that needs to change
but the backdrop of sight

the notion of clarity
where there is none

A shard in your tire
waylays us on this
the most glorious of days

Nothing to do but walk
and that you cannot do

The bike sequestered behind a tree
we wait for a vessel
to bring us home

weary but welcome

glad for a little wear and tear

But when we push up the daisies,
The melody! the rest is accessory

44

The plant delves into degenerative cosmetics
the cause of more than one argument
a month of frenzied staff meetings

I pursue my own line
of logic to the end
neighbors and naysayers be damned

Across the table
fallacious conclusions and unencumbered assumptions
mark their method of attack

It all ends up at the landfill

                          pots and barrels and cans
                          our invention near completion

The plant reshifts priorities
returns to shredding trees

*The company is constantly
experimenting on its own people.*

A top-down directive
requires a shuffling of cubicles

Farewell faithful smokestack!
Farewell tower of the freshly cut!
Air redolent of pulp and death!
Farewell farewell farewell!

Eleven rows of cars my new vista
their gleam and window glare
their histories laid bare to me
my Daily Journal of Heretofore Unknown Events
ready to be filled

No one to ignore me
once I'm through

(what a stink, what a wonderful smell)

Woe to him from Sector C
who keyed the Nissan 300Z
and sneaked away so sneakily

Woe to the visitor
on a visitor's pass
who upon leaving
made a right angle
of your antenna

Woe to the pigeons
nesting in that lamp
guano splattering
the Director's Lincoln
with precision

I want to believe the beautiful lies
the past spreads out like a feast.

Blond hair on your overcoat

The situation revolves on itself

Stasis   action   guilt

It's the first that hurts
the last that reminds us
we're here

This house is full of toxins

How late we came into the story
not as protagonists but as props

But to be an extra
adds an angle to these lives

"Alouah   Alouah   Alouah"

a store of words
you will not hear me say

The day   that anaconda
twists through the motions
8 to 5 then back again

A huge day   swollen
with what it swallows

                                400 people on the premises

mouth broken open
a manhole without its cover

Those depths hide more than one rat

a second is a killing thing

We strive for the effluvium
but lack all requisite lightness
find ourselves squarely placed
in the fluorescence of the feebly salaried

No lack of glory will redeem
this tendency toward failure
wayward intentions   insinuations
lives we circle and occasionally probe

Stasis   action   guilt
a common scene   a game almost
in its three-stepness   its crisp order

Would trade it for nothing
not an office with walls
not a callipygian receptionist

This motion subsumes all the rest

Everything I do passes through a narrow door,
And the door seems rather heavy.

Seeming to be a part of things
this talking around the subject

a refusal to acknowledge
the supremacy of the subject

we lilt and caper around the plant
each cubicle a vessel   no   a draft

that lifts our words to the ceiling tiles
not like smoke   no movement visible

not spiritual or even emotional
but they're up there   blending

long after we release them
acting the parts we refuse to play

nothing happens and this
is paradise

All this talk of last rites
last will and testament
witnesses and final wishes

has cost us more than one
pair of friends

I clean all flat surfaces

                              the range
                              the sink
                              microwave top
                              book of hours
                              pile of numbers

The pipes burst last night

I spit and spit
on the mop head

The swatter hangs on its nail
a newly aborted mission

"A hot plate can change your life"
you say   stranded on the counter
waiting for the beef brisket to thaw

Do you hear what I'm telling you?

Sexual mores shelved
the night was one to remember
one to remember

Moiré   cotton balls
all sorts of flashy fabrics
scattered on the floor
and furniture for days after

the neighbors' looks
neither condemning nor knowing
but vacant   hardly curious

You wish you could call
the sounds back

                    "meant for no one's ears"

But they're gone
you and I released them
into the space
between our unit and theirs
that fire wall

In fact, what change?

"Sewage is always sewage
no matter how you dress it up"

"Those poor poor children"

I want a pool view
not this Winnebago on blocks

We climb the chainlink
for the lifeguard chair

I ascend   lean backward
afraid to flirt with concrete

"Perhaps a decision is in order"
you yell from the water

Who can save you from drowning
now that I am sidelined?

Who

if not I?

Sources

More Dangerous Than Dying
—Brynne Rebele-Henry

You have been this way
and I am following.
—Peter Rose, "Shaft"

did flaunt
every asset we had
—J.H. Prynne, "Triodes, Book III"

Late September is a choking furnace.
—James Merrill, *The Book of Ephraim*

a little mission
fraught with anchors
—Jean Donnelly, "Anthem"

There is too much air in the air.
—Louis Zukofsky, "A"-12

Excess punishes me, never forgives.
—Donald Revell, "Bal des Ardents"

suffering my eye to follow
—Tom Clark, "A Winter Day"

a clear human voice
I have been afraid of ever since
—Travis Nichols, "Florida"

Solace is found in sameness
—John Yau, "Bowery Studio"

Amidst this haste and filth
—John Yau, "Russian Letter (6)"

"I," I mused, "yes, I"
—James Schuyler, "Wonderful World"

The light at least was not to be dismissed.
—William Bronk, "The Annihilation of Matter"

I repeat things in order to feel them.
—Henri Cole, "Middle Earth"

NOTHING is exactly what we do.
—James Merrill, *The Book of Ephraim*

The no, not, never,
not even, nothing of the day.
The nothing, nada, no thing,
not now of morning.
—Peter Gizzi, "Beacon"

My chatter is meant to distract
you from my ignorance.
—Beth Anderson, "A Rare Creature"

outside, melting white paper
—Andrea Brady, "Liberties, the City Adorned like a Bride"

The stench stinks.
—James Schuyler, "The Cenotaph"

You go to bed a failure and rise a saint
—Gig Ryan, "Autumn"

But when we push up the daisies,
The melody! the rest is accessory
—Louis Zukofsky, "A"-6

The company is constantly
                experimenting on its own people.
—Louis Zukofsky, "A"-8

(what a stink, what a wonderful smell)
—James Schuyler, "An East Window on Elizabeth Street"

I want to believe the beautiful lies
the past spreads out like a feast.
—John Forbes, "Watching the Treasurer"

This house is full of toxins
—Gig Ryan, "Advent"

a store of words
you will not hear me say
—Donald Revell, "The Gaza of Winter"

a second is a killing thing
—C. D. Wright, "Clockmaker with Bad Eyes"

Everything I do passes through a narrow door,
And the door seems rather heavy.
—Medbh McGuckian, "The Partner's Desk"

nothing happens and this
is paradise
—Robert Adamson, "The white abyss"

Do you hear what I'm telling you?
—C. D. Wright, "Clockmaker with Bad Eyes"

In fact, what change?
—Richard Kenney, "The Hours of the Day"

The Stripping Point

Decide on deciduous or remain ever green

My love   for envy is not your color

Today   un dieu des mauvais cheveux

Medusa could use a snaky excuse

Hotwired straight to the stripping point

Vanishment in ravishment will produce a

Rather than begin with "the day"

And its "attendant anxieties"

Disappointments   perverse

-Ities   we'll call on something else

(No wonder allowed in these pages

No wonder the pages allow it) to travesty

The burden of the day extends itself night-

Ward   marl of munificence   sutured sounds

Reverberate in the oubliette of obligation

The nocturne drops into gear   down- then

Upshift   and the song asserts itself

Impossible arias foundering on the shore

A blanket of blankets swarms the bed

Ten degrees and cropping   six sheets to the wind

The door frame chipped and tawdry

Who succumbs to coming   twice in an evening

Tram or bus   tram or bus   tram or bus   tram

Or bus   tram or bus   tram or bus   tram

Paralysis cystidian   not -like or -esque

This matter of suffixes suffices

To entice us   your proofreader on leave

My duties delight us   the nightcapping bunch

Who sink into the couch's cushions

Well into dawn   crease-ridden and louse-

Some days the tongue needs a prophylactic

Contusion me blue   confluence of lung-

Less bodies   less impact than palaver

Stupefy the progeny   do it for prosperity

The children frying in cast iron skillets

Beachfront propriety so up this season

You perform your duties to the state

Dust can't even touch down   a top-

Secret mission   you stay up late

I forget who the villain is   what he's done

Slide the pepper grinder across that distance

A mosquito falls.   stunned with blood

Your nival ambitions have snowed us in

This corpus an accomplice in pinguescence

Talk of ebb and flow   a riparian existence

Nothing is further from the stretched truth

Nothing pleases you more than the cat's shaved tail

The chinchilla on its wheel   the chinchilla   on its wheel

A nod and whisper carry the day into sweat-

Drenched dark   the one wave lolling at the sand

Oiled and ready you forgot the requisite towel

And novel   shiver under the

A snow day in the park   your trousseau

Weaving theopathy into the daily fabric

Guidance offered held in abeyance

Drudgery puffs itself up into tragedy

To flare   ignite hindrance from happiness

A streak of terror   absence sans serif

Arc of letter upon letter upon

Strung alphabet   fount of all fonts

Leaves soak in the gutter for want

Of attention   the sparrows tattered

With buckshot sear their own Cavalerius

Into the lawn   plastic spoons whittled to spears

Aspill across the floor   pen knives

Arrive by the bucket   (to) spread skinward

The lantern distracts spectacle from soreness

Cause of waiting before the week ends

Altar to fracture   burnt wagers

Tinderbox kindled letter by letter   the launch

Across valleys   sad news for the stars

Surrender to dim and be done with darkness

Delicious and made with desire from desire

Maddened and mast-bound in distress and out-

Bound   it's touch-and-go   a no-holds-barred

Affair   take care with your ticket   take your ticket

To bed   be dazzling darling   be darling

Sizzling and scathing   the long way to

Rather than begin with "the day"

The door frame chipped and tawdry

The lantern distracts spectacle from soreness

Well into dawn   crease-ridden and louse-

Ward   marl of munificence   sutured sounds

Aspill across the floor   pen knives

Hotwired straight to the stripping point

Stupefy the progeny   do it for prosperity

This corpus an accomplice in pinguescence

Delicious and made with desire from desire

Oiled and ready you forgot the requisite towel

A mosquito falls   stunned with blood

A streak of terror   absence sans serif

And its attendant anxieties

Nothing is further from the stretched truth

Across valleys sad news for the stars

Weaving theopathy into the daily fabric

Contusion me blue   confluence of lung

My love   for envy is not your color

Dust can't even touch down   a top-

Strung alphabet   fount of all fonts
Sizzling and scathing the long way to
Disappointments   perverse
Arrive by the bucket to spread skinward
Upshift and the song asserts itself

The children frying in cast iron skillets

Ten degrees and cropping   six sheets to the wind

A snow day in the park   your trousseau

Maddened and mast-bound in distress and out

To entice us   your proofreader on leave

Vanishment in ravishment will produce a

Talk of ebb and flow   a riparian existence

Leaves soak in the gutter for want

Drudgery puffs itself up into tragedy

I forget who the villain is   what he's done

Altar to fracture   burnt wagers

Who sink into the couch's cushions

With buckshot   sear their own Cavalerius

To flare   ignite hindrance from happiness

The burden of the day extends itself   night

The chinchilla on its wheel   the chinchilla on its wheel

This matter of suffixes suffices

Medusa could use a snaky excuse

Who succumbs to coming twice in an evening

Some days the tongue needs a prophylactic

No wonder the pages allow it to travesty

The nocturne drops into gear   down then

Drenched dark   the one wave lolling at the sand

Tram or bus   tram or bus   tram or bus   tram

Affair   take care with your ticket   take your ticket

Secret mission   you stay up late

Surrender to dim and be done with darkness

Paralysis cystidian not -like or -esque

Today un dieu des mauvais cheveux

Guidance offered held in abeyance

Nothing pleases you more than the cat's shaved tail

A blanket of blankets swarms the bed

Impossible arias foundering on the shore-

Less bodies   less impact than palaver

A nod and whisper carry the day into sweat

Weaving theopathy into the daily fabric

The lantern distracts spectacle from soreness

Well into dawn   crease-ridden and louse-

Maddened and mast-bound in distress and out

Upshift and the song asserts itself

Tram or bus   tram or bus   tram or bus   tram

Drenched dark   the one wave lolling at the sand

And its attendant anxieties

Hotwired straight to the stripping point

A mosquito falls   stunned with blood

Sizzling and scathing the long way to

Talk of ebb and flow   a riparian existence

Dust can't even touch down atop

The chinchilla   on its wheel   the chinchilla on its wheel

A streak of terror   absence sans serif

Across valleys   sad news for the stars

To flare   ignite hindrance from happiness
Delicious and made with desire from desire
A blanket of blankets swarms the bed
My love   for envy is not your color

The door frame chipped and tawdry

Aspill across the floor   pen knives

Oiled and ready   you forgot the requisite towel

Contusion me blue   confluence of lung

Who succumbs to coming twice in an evening

A nod and whisper carry the day into sweat

Surrender to dim and be done with darkness

Medusa could use a snaky excuse

No wonder the pages allow it   to travesty

A snow day in the park   your trousseau

This matter of suffixes suffices

Leaves soak in the gutter for want

The nocturne drops into gear   down then

Some days the tongue needs a prophylactic

Vanishment in ravishment will produce a

"Rather than begin with 'the day'"

Nothing is further from the stretched truth

Who sink into the couch's cushions

The burden of the day extends itself   night-

Less bodies less impact than palaver

Impossible arias foundering on the shore

Guidance offered held in abeyance

Altar to fracture   burnt wagers

Arrive by the bucket to spread skinward

Talk of ebb and flow   a riparian existence

Sizzling and scathing the long way to

Less bodies   less impact than palaver

Oiled and ready you forgot the requisite towel

The chinchilla on its wheel   the chinchilla on its wheel

A nod and whisper carry the day into sweat

Hotwired straight to the stripping point

A blanket of blankets swarms the bed

Surrender to dim and be done with darkness

This matter of suffixes suffices

No wonder the pages allow it to travesty

My love   for envy is not your color

Tram or bus   tram or bus   tram or bus   tram

Impossible arias foundering on the shore

Dust can't even touch down   a top

The door frame chipped and tawdry

Medusa could use a snaky excuse

And its attendant anxieties

The burden of the day extends itself   night

Weaving theopathy into the daily fabric

To flare   to ignite hindrance from happiness

Across valleys   sad news for the stars

Who sink into the couch's cushions

A mosquito falls   stunned with blood

Contusion me blue   confluence of lung-

Some days   the tongue needs a prophylactic

Delicious and made with desire from desire

Arrive by the bucket to spread skinward

Nothing is further from the stretched truth

The lantern distracts spectacle from soreness

This matter of suffixes suffices

My love   for envy is not your color

The chinchilla   on its wheel   the chinchilla on its wheel

Weaving theopathy into the daily fabric

Nothing is further from the stretched truth

Dust can't even touch down atop

Less bodies   less impact than palaver

A blanket of blankets swarms the bed

Sizzling and scathing the long way to

To flare   ignite hindrance from happiness

Some days the tongue needs a prophylactic

Medusa could use a snaky excuse

Impossible arias foundering on the shore

Across valleys   sad news for the stars

Hotwired straight to the stripping point

A mosquito falls   stunned with blood

A nod and whisper carry the day into sweat

Surrender to dim and be done with darkness

About the Author

Brian Henry is the author of four previous books of poetry: *Astronaut* (2000), *American Incident* (2002), *Graft* (2003), and *Quarantine* (2006). His poems have appeared in many magazines around the world, including *Jacket, New American Writing, American Poetry Review, Boston Review,* and *Volt.* He has coedited *Verse* since 1995, and he coedited *The Verse Book of Interviews* (2005). He currently teaches literature and creative writing at the University of Richmond in Virginia.